T0132058

A
VOICE
IN THE
KINGDOM

By Wanda Liddell

AuthorHouse™
1663 Liberty Drive
Bloomington, IN 47403
www.authorhouse.com
Phone: 1 (800) 839-8640

KJV
Scripture quotations marked KJV are from the Holy Bible, King James Version (Authorized Version). First published
in 1611. Quoted from the KJV Classic Reference Bible, Copyright © 1983 by The Zondervan Corporation.

ISBN: 978-1-7283-2361-9 (sc)
ISBN: 978-1-7283-2362-6 (e)

Print information available on the last page.

Published by AuthorHouse 09/11/2019

authorHOUSE®

Acknowledgement

I would like to thank a few people that helped me along the way. Apostle Rod and Prophetess Selena for always being there for me through prayers, encouragement, and whatever else was needed.

Sis. Dequecha, you were tremendous with helping me to put things in order, explaining what I didn't know. You are truly an amazing gift from God; your talents, skills, and abilities.

Jennifer and LaRonda, a big thanks to you.

Cora, thank you for pointing me to the right person and your friendship.

Prophetess Ann for pushing and praying for me to finish.

Steve and Elijah for all the extra time I needed to do this.

To my natural family, remember you have a voice to be used not for yourself, but others as well. You make a difference.

Table of Contents

INTRODUCTION

I've always known that I have a loud, booming, and boisterous voice.

What can I say, it runs in my bloodline. I come from a family of seven whose parents believed in education and instilled in us that we can be anything in life that we want with a little hard work. Outside of my siblings, our family is very large, and I remember many family gatherings. Growing up, it was definitely loud...ha-ha. Some of them were not as loud, but the majority ruled.

When I graduated from high school, I chose at that time not to attend college. Instead, I struck out on my own and began to live life in the fast lane. I became caught up in drugs in my early twenties, which spiraled into 12 years of my life. While I was out there, people would always say I hear you before I can see you. That statement rang true but irritated me; nonetheless, I didn't care at the time and continued doing what I wanted, when I wanted, and how I wanted.

While I was doing my own thing at the hang-out place, I had a friend that I would signal just by using my voice from one end of the street to the other. He would hear me call his name and come whistling and running towards me because he knew something was up. When I began to come to my senses some years later, I knew that there was a better life than what I was living. I moved to Michigan and got the help I needed. It was at this time I gave my heart over to the Lord and sought help from a faith-based ministry called Teen Challenge. Here I am 28 years later still free from my old life; thanks to an encounter with Jesus showing me a better way of life and learning how to overcome.

My voice remains just as loud. As I continued in this new direction in my life, people still made mention of my voice. As I grew in the things of God, I learned that I was a voice in God's Kingdom.

CHAPTER ONE

BE YOURSELF

As I continued my Christian walk with the Lord, it seemed more and more people would have something to say about my loudness. I didn't understand why. After all, I thought I couldn't help it and that I was made this way and I could be as loud as I want to be. I was sensitive about it at times, it really bothered me, and I found myself being offended by others when it came to my voice.

I began to get interested in the food Industry and felt a desire to go to college for Culinary Arts. God increased that desire within me. I found myself signing up for classes to attend. I tell you, even at school I couldn't even escape the comments and jokes about my voice.

One day while in school, I decided that I was going to become someone else (notice I said I). I started by being really quiet and talking low. This went on for about three to four days. Funny thing was people thought I was sick or something was wrong. God placed a dear Christian friend, whom has gone home to be with the Lord, in my path while attending school from the very first day. He called me into his office and asked me what was going on. He noticed I was trying to be someone else. I was not being my usual bubbly self. He ministered to me out of Jeremiah 29:11 and reminded me to be me and allow God to critique me and not people. I must say I learned a valuable lesson that day.

CHAPTER TWO

PURPOSE AND FREEDOM

One particular Sunday as I was attending my home church, I sat right up in the front row, which is something I don't normally do. As I listened to the Pastor's message that day, there was something special about the message as if it was designed particularly for me (God will do that). That day was chosen by God to help me begin to understand that my voice has a purpose and he is going to use it for his glory.

According to Psalm 139:14, I was fearfully, and wonderfully created by his hands, and Isaiah 24:44 says He formed me from the womb.

I cried as God's revelation began to unfold and help me to understand the journey of learning my voice. I now needed to learn how to use my voice by being softer or louder.

CHAPTER THREE

THE ENCOUNTERS OF OTHERS

I continued on this journey of learning about my loud, booming and boisterous voice. I found that I wasn't alone as there were others just like me that I hadn't really noticed before (funny how that works after revelation)! They had the same loudness, some more than others. I didn't see them as loud, I saw them as a voice in the kingdom of God that needed to be tamed and trained.

Many people know that there is value in their voice that could save or destroy a life. Proverbs 18:21 says death and life are in the power of the tongue: and they that love it shall eat the fruit thereof. Being careful how we use our voice is important to understand; especially when ministering to people because we never know where they are or what they are going through in life.

CHAPTER FOUR

SPEAK UP! YOUR VOICE MATTERS

I want to know why we don't speak up when we should? I believe it's because we sometimes allow the enemy to influence us with a spirit of fear. Fear stops us in our tracks. It causes us to be paralyzed and stagnates our growth. 2 Timothy 1:7 says God has not given us this spirit. Fear keeps our mouths shut when we should be speaking up to what God tells us to say. Fear makes us think about the "what if's". What if I mess up? What if I say the wrong thing? Fear makes us question whether it's God or ourselves speaking to us.

We have God's heart at best when we spend time with him in prayer and the word. We get His mind and heart in those times of seeking Him. We have the mind of Christ! You are made in his image! The word confirms this statement in Phil 2:5 - Let this mind be in you which was also in Christ Jesus.

As one who has been called and chosen to be a voice in the kingdom, I've been in that place of fear, and at moments still do. But, I have to do it afraid by stepping out and doing and saying what thus says the Lord, and going where he sends me. I realize every day that fear is not the spirit God gave me. I'm an overcomer who walks with boldness, victory, strength and power with Him.

CHAPTER FIVE

MEGAPHONE

A megaphone is defined as a device for amplifying and directing the voice.

The word amplify means to increase the volume, to expand, or enlarge.

I believe that some of us have built-in amplifiers where we don't need a microphone. When we want to, we are able to increase and expand the sound of our voice to be heard in a crowd.

From my understanding, the way our voice works there are certain parts that help us to produce sound when we speak or sing.

1. Lungs are the power.
2. The voice box projects sound.
3. Throat, nose, mouth and sinus all play a part. Air also plays a large part when we exhale and inhale.

We really are made perfect by the hand of God. He knew what he was doing. We have the ability to not just talk loud but sing loud as well.

I've said all of this to bring clarity as we continue with this chapter so you will understand where I am going.

I used to hang out at a certain spot when I was living life in the fast lane doing drugs, alcohol and weed. I had a hangout buddy. We hung out together at the spot. I would yell his name from one end of the block to half way down the street where he was and he would respond back with a whistle. That's how loud my voice would amplify.

Some people struggle with the loudness or softness of their voice. Some people have a soft voice and don't like it at all. They yell as loud as they possibly can and their voice still can't be heard. On the other hand, take someone like me and it's like Merrill Lynch (ha ha).

My point is the enemy will try to shut us down by using our insecurities against us whether loud or soft. We get offended when someone says something about our voice.

I'm here to let you know that you are a voice in the kingdom and for some of us a very loud voice. So let's stop trying to be someone else and be who God called us to be.

Say the following statement with me, "I'm loud/soft yet a voice in God's kingdom with his purpose and assignment".

Your voice is assigned to people, so don't allow it to be shut down. You are cheating yourself and someone else for what God desires to say through you.

Again, repeat after me, "I'm confident in who God called me to be and do. I will speak up and speak out and bind devils and help set the captives free".

God knew what he was doing when he created us.

CHAPTER SIX

CAN YOU SPEAKER LOUDER PLEASE!

Some of us were created to talk softer. This does not diminish our kingdom value. They are just not as loud as others. It's okay! A soft voice can calm people down and even stop someone from committing suicide because of the softness of tone. I'm here to let you know you're a voice in the Kingdom on the soft side. To be honest, I never really thought about it much until I started writing this book.

You are the voice that helps bring balance like good cop/bad cop (smile). Don't force yourself to be loud or mimic others. You have your portion and place in the kingdom. Be confident!

One of my former jobs consisted of daily cooking in a school. Well, when I had to put student numbers in the computer as they passed through the line, I constantly had to ask students to speak up (especially in the morning). This made me question my hearing, but I soon realized that was their voice to be heard. As a matter of fact, one student let me know that it was how they always talked. I remember so well many that were soft spoken yet confident in who they were with their unique voices making a difference in the lives of others.

CHAPTER SEVEN

4 TYPES OF VOICES

....

(Which one are you?)

I've come to notice there are at least 4 types of voices.

Soft Voices- These type of people talk softly no matter how much you ask them to speak up. Their voice will tend to remain the same. It's just the way they are created to speak.

Screamers-These people are just natural born screamers. They scream even when there just talking. It's that way whether praying or talking. There is always a scream type of sound coming out of their voice box, and yes, at times it's irritating! There is no way around it, and we have to accept them for who they simply are.

Yellers- These people just yell about any and everything. This is how they talk and express themselves to get a point across. They sometimes yell throughout the day. You might even tell them to stop yelling, yet they will reply with a difference of opinion because they do not even realize they are yelling.

LOUD- This one probably describe me best (smile if It's you)! If you're reading this book and loud describes you, we are just LOUD. We are heard before we are ever seen. You might as well come to grips with it. It's okay! It's a part of our character, but we do know how to tame it when necessary.

So, don't ever try to be someone you are not. Use your God given voice. I can't be you and you can't be me. Do we adapt and adjust when it's needed? Yes, absolutely!

If this is you, learn how to calm your voice to cater to the circumstance. We have to know when is the right time to tone our voices down. God will help and train us if we are willing to be pliable. He will use others to help us recognize that we need that balance to tone it down; especially if we are not a soft voice.

Which one are you, now that you have something to go on? Be willing to realize if you need to allow your voice to shift its frequency.

CHAPTER EIGHT

FINDING PURPOSE IN YOUR VOICE

John the Baptist was one who cried out in the wilderness.

A forerunner of voices, he knew the purpose of his voice was to proclaim the coming Jesus. John was born to do one of many things. One was to let his voice be heard. He came to proclaim with his voice and bring a message of repentance because the Kingdom was at hand. Matt 3:2

He also came to cry out for preparation for the way of the Lord. He baptized in the Jordan River people from Judea, Jerusalem, and surrounding regions to help bring about repentance of sin.

The greatest way was the baptizing of Jesus by John. In all this, John was still using his voice to do what it was purposed for.

Conclusion

I've come to the final conclusion that my voice was destined. I was born, created, and fearfully and wonderfully made by the hands of God to be a voice. I am a voice not only in the Kingdom but in the earth as well to proclaim the good news of the gospel, sing His songs, pray the word, intercede for people, and encourage. I am a prophetic voice of order and justice. My voice is unique! My voice was created for greatness and to bring a spark of hope and enlightenment of His awesomeness and greatness.

There are three major questions we need to ask ourselves so we know we are a voice in the Kingdom.

1. How do I find my purpose for my voice?
2. How do I know my identity for my voice?
3. Does my voice matter and why?

When we can answer these three questions, then we will begin to understand and know the purpose for our voice.

Printed in the United States
By Bookmasters